Praise for "Doggy Finds Her Bone"
『わんこが骨を見つける』の称賛

"The combination of pictures and plot in Doggy Finds Her Bone offers a perfect opportunity for a grandfather (or grandmother) to share with a grandchild too young to read on his or her own. The search of a beautiful dog hunting for a bone in the typical American home is a story familiar to every young child. The author's questions - tailored for a young mind – encourages interaction between the reader and child beyond the written words, transforming simple entertainment into a shared learning experience for both. It's a perfect story to share with a Grandchild! Every grandparent should own the books from Ella the Doggy book series!"   William Forsythe, III

「『わんこが骨を見つける』の写真と内容の組み合わせは、祖父（または祖母）が孫と一緒に読むには、絶好の機会を提供します。 典型的なアメリカの家で骨を探す綺麗な犬のお話は、すべての幼い子供に親しまれている物語です。作者の質問 - 若い心に合わせた物 - 書かれている内容を超えて読者と子供の関係を促進でき、単純な娯楽が共有学習体験に変わります。孫と共有するのに最適な物語です。 すべての祖父母は『わんこのエラ』のブックシリーズを買うべきです！」– ウィリアム・フォーサイス、III

"Doggy Finds Her Bone" is a cute story of perseverance and how trying harder has its rewards. A very enjoyable book to read, which includes the added bonus of a very subtle lesson for young children and a good reminder for adults about perseverance!" Mavis Winkels

「『わんこが骨を見つける』は、とてもかわいい物語で忍耐力の受容性を伝えてくれます。一生懸命努力すると必ず報われる事を教えてくれます。 子供と一緒に読んで楽しめる本で、人生に重要な忍耐力について教えてくれます。また、大人にも忍耐力の重要性を思い出させます！」 – メイビス・ウィンケルズ

"Doggy Finds Her Bone" is a cute book about a silly dog who can't remember where she left her bone. She searches everywhere she can think that it might be. Not only is this book a great read for all generations, it also teaches us about determination and to never give up. This book draws readers in and opens up discussion for everyone to become involved in the story. An instant classic that will open the hearts of everyone who reads this book!"   Heather Howell

「『わんこが骨を見つける』は、どこに骨を置いたか思い出せないちょっとおバカな犬の物語です。エラは、骨があるかもしれないと思う場所を全て検索します。この本はすべての世代に素晴らしい本であり、決意や決してあきらめないことについても教えてくれます。ストーリー内の議論は、読者を引き込みます。この本を読んだすべての人の心を開くインスタントクラシックです！」 – ヘザー・ハウエル

"*Doggy Finds Her Bone* "is dedicated to my husband.
「わんこが骨を見つける」は私の夫に捧げます。

Ella (the doggy) and Jayne (the author)

Husky Publishing
727 11th Street NW; East Grand Forks, MN 56721
email: djflaagan@gra.midco.net

ジェイン・フラーガンのウェブサイトはこちらから：www.ellathedoggy.com
連絡はこちらからも受け付けております：djflaagan@gra.midco.net

2014 年出版。文章、カバーデザイン、挿し絵の著作権は Jayne Flaagan に帰属します。）
© 2014 Jayne Flaagan Cover Design © 2014 Jayne Flaagan, photography by Jayne Flaagan

著者からの書面による許可なく、本書の全部または一部の無断複写、あらゆる検索システムでの保存、コピー・スキャン・その他手段でのデジタル化等による譲渡並びに配信など、著者の権利を侵害する行為は一切禁止されています。Copyright © 2014 Jayne Flaagan Cover Design © 2014 Jayne Flaagan Pictures by Jayne Flaagan（or, 2014 年出版。文章、カバーデザイン、写真の著作権は Jayne Flaagan に帰属します。）

No part of this publication may be reproduced in whole or in part, or stored in a retrieval system, or transmitted in any form or by any means, electronic, mechanical, photocopying, recording or otherwise, without written permission of the author.

One day Ella the Doggy got a treat.
あるひ、わんこのエラがおかしをもらいました。

It was a bone that she could chew.
エラがかんでたのしめるためのほねでした。

Ella liked her treat and she quickly gobbled it up!
エラはこのおかしがだいすきで、すぐにたべました！

Then Ella remembered something.
そしたらエラはなにかをおもいだしました。

She remembered that she had an even BIGGER bone!
もっとおおきなほねをもっていることをおもいだしました！

This is a picture of the bone.
これが、ほねのしゃしんです。

Look at how big it is!
すごくおおきいね！

But Ella had a problem.
でも、エラにはもんだいがありました。

She could not remember where she had left her very big bone!
おおきなほねをどこにおいたかおもいだせません！

So she went to look for it.
だからエラは、ほねをさがしにいきました。

The first place that Ella looked for her bone was behind the kitchen door.

さいしょにエラがほねをさがしいったばしょは、キッチンのドアのうしろでした。

Did she find her bone there? No, she did not!
そこでほねをみつけましたか？ ざんねん！みつかりませんでした

Then Ella bent way far down and
looked under the refrigerator.
そしたらエラは、れいぞうこのしたをみてみました。

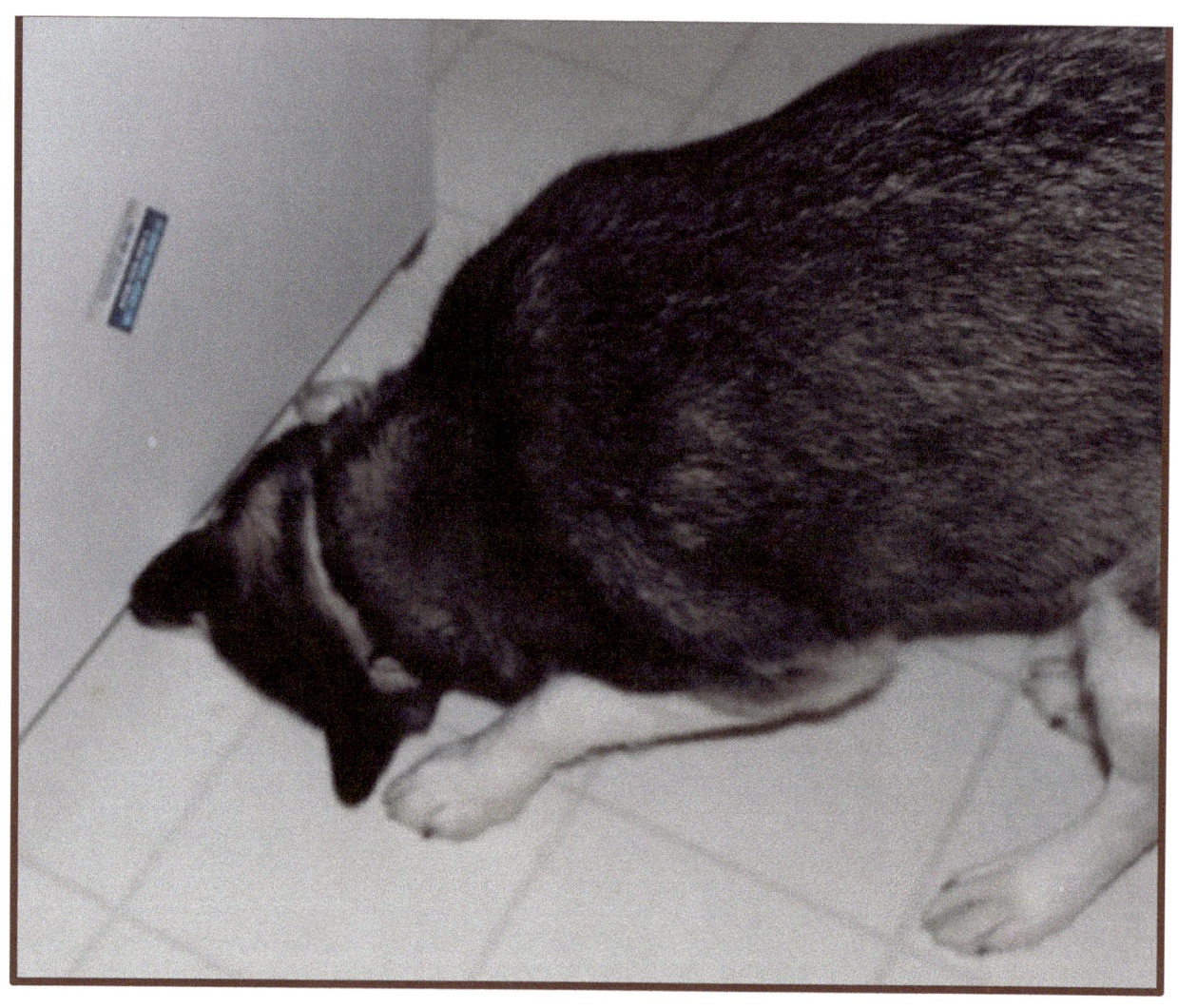

But the bone was not there either.
でも、ほねはそこにもありませんでした。

Next, Ella looked under the sofa in the living room.
つぎに、エラはリビングのソファのしたをみてみました。

**The sofa had lots of pretty pink
and blue flowers...but no bone.**

ソファーにはきれいなピンクとあおのはながたくさんありましたが、
ほねは、ありませんでした。

After that, Ella looked by the pretty green plant.
そのあと、エラはきれいなみどりいろのしょくぶつをみつめました。

Poor Ella!
エラがかわいそう！

She still has not found her bone.
まだほねをみつけられません。

Then Ella went all the way down the hallway
to look in the bathroom.

そしたらエラは、ろうかをずっとあるいておふろにたどりつきました。

All she found was a pink wash cloth in the bathtub.

でも、おふろにあったのはピンクのせんたくぬのでした。

Ella even looked for her bone in a stinky black shoe!
エラは、くさいくろいくつのなかもさがしました！

What a silly place to look for a bone!
ほねをさがすには、おかしいばしょだね。

Ella had looked all over the house for her big, juicy bone.
エラは、おおきくてジューシーなほねをいえじゅうさがしました。

Where do you think she looked next?
つぎは、どこをさがしたとおもう？

You are right if you guessed that Ella went to look outside!
エラがそとをみにいったとおもったらだいせいこう！

When she got outside, Ella looked for her bone in a flower pot.
そとにでると、エラはうえきばちをみてみました。

There was just some stones and a little green apple in the pot.
そこには、いしとあおリンゴしかはいっていませんでした。

Do you like to eat apples? Do you eat stones?
きみは、りんごをたべますか？ いしをたべますか？

Ella looked under the steps next...and under a fir tree,
つぎにエラは、かいだんのした、そしてモミのきのしたをみました

but she still could not find the bone.
でも、まだほねをみつけることができません。

When Ella looked on the blue ladder,
she saw something very small on one of the steps.
エラがあおいはしごをみると、そこにとてもちさいものがみえました。

Can you see it? It was a berry and Ella ate it!
みえるかな？　そこにはベリーがあって、エラはそれをたべました！

The swimming pool was the next place Ella looked.
つぎにエラは、プールをみてみました。

Do you like to swim?
きみはおよぐのは、すき？

Ella looked on the swing too.
エラは、ブランコもみました。

She found a few leaves that had fallen from a tree...but no bone.
きからおちたはっぱをいくつかみつけましたが、
ほねは、ありません！

Do you see that the swing looks like the American flag?
ブランコがアメリカのこっきのようにみえる？

Ella did not find her bone by the back garage either.
ガレージでもほねをみつけれませんでした。

Do you think Ella is ever going to find her treat?
エラは、ほねをみつけられるとおもいますか？

Here is Ella thinking about where else
she could look for her bone.
エラはここで、どこをさがせばほねがあるか、かんがえています。

She thinks, "mmm...maybe my bone is by
the raspberry bushes."
「うーん……わたしのほねは、ラズベリーのきにあるかな。」

But no, the bone was not by the raspberry bushes.
でも、ラズベリーのきには

Ella was getting very hot and tired.
エラは、もうあつくてつかれていました。

Her tongue is hanging out because that is how doggies cool off when they get too warm.
エラのしたがでてるのは、
いぬがあつくなるとすずしくなるためにそうするからです。

How do you stay cool?
あなたは、どうやってすずしくなりますか？

Poor Ella! She did not know where else to look for her bone.
エラがかわいそう！もうどこをみればいいかわかりません。

She decided to go to her doggy house and rest for a bit.
エラは、いえにいき、すこしやすむことにしました。

Ella's house is inside a kennel.
エラのいえは、いぬごやのなかにあります。

A kennel is a house for a dog or a cat.
いぬごやは、いぬやねこようのいえです。

Where do you live?
あなたは、どこにすんでいますか？

When Ella got to her house, there was something inside!
エラがいえについたら、なかになにかがありました！

Do you see what it is? Do you think Ella sees it too?
きみもみえるかな？ エラもみえるかな？

Her bone is inside her doggy house!
エラのほねがいぬごやにありました！

Ella the doggy has found her bone!
わんこのエラがやっとほねをみつけました！

This doggy has worked very hard!
このわんこは、いっしょうけんめいがんばりました！

She did not stop looking for her bone until she found it.
ほねをみつけるまであきらめませんでした！

Good job Ella!
がんばったね、エラ！

How do you think Ella feels now that she has found her bone?
エラは、やっとほねをみつけてどうおもってるのかな？

Yes, Ella is a very, very happy doggy!
ほんとうにエラはとてもしあわせないぬです！

Jayne Flaagan grew up in North Dakota and made the big move to Minnesota many years ago. She lives with her husband and her goofy dog named Ella. She also has three adult children.

Flaagan has degrees in Advertising/Public Relations, Elementary Education and French. Her experience includes a background of over 30 years in Elementary and Early Childhood education, as well an extensive expertise in writing for many different publications and in several different genres. She thoroughly enjoys writing for young readers.

The author can speak Spanish, loves to travel, read, do crossword puzzles, and spend time with her family, as well as having various other hobbies and past times.

Books have always been a huge part of her life and reading to children is something that she feels is critical to every child's learning experience. Between her jobs and raising her children, she estimates that she has probably read over a million books to children over the years!

Ella is the second husky that she and her family have had the joy of including in the family. Ella has provided so much joy and entertainment for her own family that Flaagan decided she wanted to share Ella with other families. Thus, "Ella the Doggy" book series was born!

ジェーン・フラガンはノースダコタ州で育ち、何年も前にミネソタ州に引っ越しました。彼女は夫とちょっとおバカな犬エラと一緒に住んでいます。彼女には、3人の子供がいます。

フラガンは、広告/広報、初等教育、そしてフランス語の学位を持っています。

彼女の経験は、小学校および幼児教育における30年以上の経歴と、多くの異なる出版物、そして異なるジャンルの執筆における広範な専門知識が含まれます。彼女は若い読者のために書く事を楽しんでいます。

作者はスペイン語を話し、旅行、読書、クロスワードパズルを愛し、家族と過ごすこと、他のさまざまな趣味があります。

本は常に彼女の人生の大部分であり、子供たちに読むことは学習経験に不可欠であると彼女が感じています。

彼女の仕事と子育ての間で、子供達には百万冊以上の本を読んだと推定しています！

エラは彼女と家族の2番目のハスキーです。エラは自分の家族に多くの喜びを与えてくれたので、フラガンはエラのお話を他の家族と共有したいと思いました。

このように、「わんこのエラ」のブックシリーズが誕生しました！

Ella the Doggy

www.ingramcontent.com/pod-product-compliance
Lightning Source LLC
Chambersburg PA
CBHW051403110526
44592CB00023B/2937